All About Money

by Natalie M. Rosinsky

Content Adviser: Jaclyn B. H. Finstad, New Ulm, Minnesota;
M.B.A., University of Findlay, Ohio

Reading Adviser: Dr. Alexa Sandmann, Professor of Literacy,
The University of Toledo; Member, International Reading Association

Let's See Library
Compass Point Books
Minneapolis, Minnesota

Compass Point Books
3109 West 50th Street, #115
Minneapolis, MN 55410

Visit Compass Point Books on the Internet at *www.compasspointbooks.com* or e-mail your
request to *custserv@compasspointbooks.com*

On the cover: A young man looks at bills at the U.S. Mint headquarters in Washington, D.C.

Photographs ©: Richard T. Nowitz, cover; Creatas, 4; Gianni Dagli Orti/Corbis, 6; Chris Hellier/Corbis, 8;
Erich Lessing/Art Resource, N.Y., 10; Courtesy of Mynthandeln.com, 12; Dennis Degnan/Corbis, 14;
Reproduced from the original held by the Department of Special Collections of the University Libraries of
Notre Dame, 16; Kevin R. Morris/Corbis, 18; Dan Dempster/Dembinsky Photo Associates, 20; John Cross/
The Free Press, 24.

Editor: Catherine Neitge
Photo Researcher: Svetlana Zhurkina
Designers: Melissa Voda/Jaime Martens

Library of Congress Cataloging-in-Publication Data
Rosinsky, Natalie M. (Natalie Myra)
 All about money / by Natalie M. Rosinsky.
     v. cm. — (Let's see library. Economics) (Let's see library)
Includes bibliographical references and index.
Contents: Why is money important? — When did people begin to use money? — What have people used as
money? — How did coins become money? — How did paper become money? — What are some other kinds
of money? — What is the story of United States money? — What are other uses for money? — What will hap-
pen to money?
 ISBN 0-7565-0482-1 (hardcover : alk. paper)
 1. Money—Juvenile literature. [1. Money.] I. Title. II. Series.
III. Series: Let's see library.
HG221.5.R67 2004
332.4—dc21   2002156023

Table of Contents

NOTE: In this book, words that are defined in the glossary
are in **bold** the first time they appear in the text.

Why Is Money Important?

The ice cream cone in your hand. The shirt on your back. The roof over your head. Money paid for all these **goods.** Perhaps you even bought that ice cream yourself!

Services you and your family use also cost money. For example, doctors and barbers are paid for their skills. Fixing roads or building schools costs a lot. The government pays for these services with **taxes** it collects.

Sunshine and smiles are free. Most other things you need every day depend on money.

◄ *A doctor checks out a young patient. The doctor is paid for her skills.*

When Did People Begin to Use Money?

Very long ago, families stayed in one place. They hunted and gathered their own food. They made their own clothing and homes. People did not need money. There was no place to spend it!

Then, people began to travel farther. Some began to farm. They had extra things they could now **barter** in markets. Was a cow worth five chickens or ten? Was sewing a coat worth a bag of wheat? People argued about the **value** of goods and services. Using money solved this problem.

◄ *Prehistoric people are shown hunting in a museum model. They did not need money.*

7

What Have People Used As Money?

Money has not always been paper bills and metal coins. Around the world, people used different things as money. They would pick something valued in their area.

Tasty salt and pretty shells were early kinds of money. Even feathers were used as money. These items could easily be lost or broken when people traveled. So, strong bars of silver or gold became money. Heavy bars were worth more. Carrying lots of money was hard work!

Going to market became easier when coins became money.

◀ *Cowrie shells were used as money.*

How Did Coins Become Money?

The first coins were **minted** in what is now Turkey. These small circles showed a lion's head. This was the sign of Turkey's king. It told people the king stood behind the worth of the coins. This money was the first **currency** of a country.

Other countries began to mint their own currency. Many traders used the owl coins of Greece.

Early coins were gold and silver. Later, coins were made of other metals. Their value was set by what was stamped on them.

◄ This silver owl coin from Greece is about 2,400 years old.

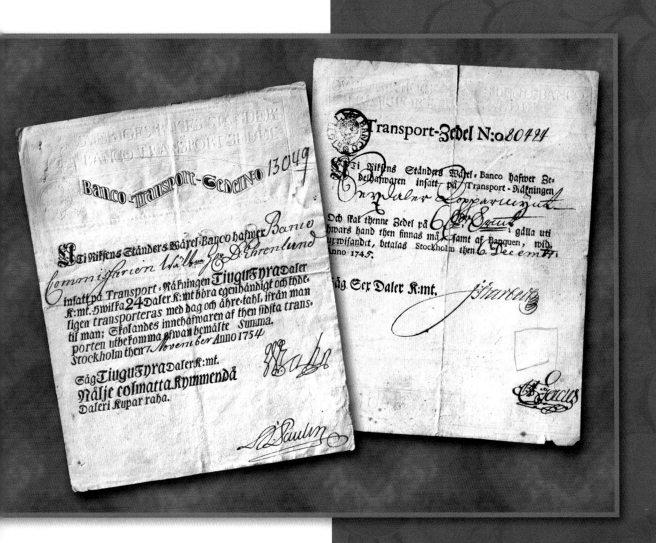

How Did Paper Become Money?

China was the first country to use paper money. Its new iron coins were heavy. Traders were glad when paper became part of the currency. China's strong government stood behind the value of each note.

In other parts of the world, governments were not as strong. People would not trust the value of paper money. They still used gold and silver coins. About 600 years passed before another country printed paper money. In 1661, Sweden added paper notes to its currency. Other countries followed.

◄ *These Swedish bank notes are from the mid-1700s.*

What Are Some Other Kinds of Money?

Sometimes, money is not currency. Money can also be special notes written by people or banks. These notes are called checks or money orders. The value of a check comes from the money a bank holds for someone. Today, many families have checking accounts with banks. Long ago, only rich people used banks this way.

People write personal checks as needed. They can be for different amounts. Money orders are a special type of check. They are paid for with currency in advance. People can get money orders at the bank, grocery store, post office, and other places.

◄ *Personal checks can be written for different amounts.*

What Is the Story of U.S. Money?

The first U.S. currency was a one cent coin. It was minted in 1787. It did not look like the penny you use today. The words "We Are One" were stamped in its middle. Thirteen circles went around its edge. They stood for the states in this new country.

Today, coins are made by the United States Mint. Paper money is printed at the Bureau of Engraving and Printing. Special paper and ink are used. These keep dishonest people from trying to **counterfeit** bills.

◄ *The first U.S. coin was minted in 1787.*

What Are Other Uses for Money?

Some people collect coins. They value coins for their age, beauty, and history. Sometimes, an unusual nickel is worth hundreds of dollars! Studying and collecting coins is called numismatics. People also collect paper money.

Money is part of our lives in other ways. It may be worn as jewelry. Pictures of money sometimes decorate clothes or homes. There are even songs and sayings about money. Busy people say that "Time is money." Were you sad to hear that "Money doesn't grow on trees"?

◄ *A woman wears a beautiful necklace decorated with coins.*

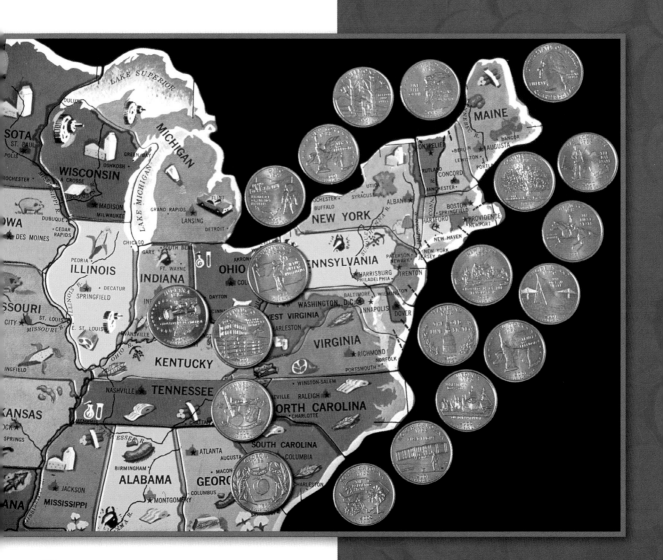

What Will Happen to Money?

Countries will continue to change their currencies. Since 1999, the United States has minted special quarters. These honor five different states each year. In 2002, twelve countries in Europe made a huge change. They began using the same, new currency. It is called the euro.

More people are using computers to pay bills. People sometimes get paid by computer, too. This kind of **electronic money** cannot be handled like coins or paper. The use of electronic money is expected to grow.

It is amazing to think how the way we use money has changed. What do you think will happen next?

◀ *Special quarters honor individual states.*

Glossary

barter—to trade something for something else

counterfeit—to make a copy of something in order to cheat people

currency—the money of a country

electronic money—money that is saved or spent by recording these changes in computer files

goods—things that are sold

minted—made into coins by stamping designs into thin pieces of metal

services—useful work

taxes—money collected and used by a government

value—what something is worth to a group of people

Did You Know?

• The new design of the $20 bill in 2003 was the first U.S. currency since 1905 to have colors other than green or black.

• On the Pacific island of Yap, people used large, round stones for money. The biggest was 12 feet (3.7 meters) wide!

• Some Native Americans used shell belts called wampum as money.

• There are more than 140 different currencies used around the world today.

• No matter what its face value, each United States bill costs four cents to print.

• Not all coins have been round. In China, early coins were shaped like axes and shovels.

• The heaviest, largest coin ever minted was the Swedish "plate dollar." It weighed 42 pounds (19 kilograms).

• When the U.S. Mint is not busy making coins for its own country, it makes them for other countries.

• Money is sometimes called bread, bucks, dough, greenbacks, lettuce, long green, and moolah.

Want to Know More?

At the Library

Maestro, Betsy. *The Story of Money.* New York: Clarion, 1993.

Parker, Nancy Winslow. *Money, Money, Money: The Meaning of the Art and Symbols on United States Paper Currency.* New York: HarperCollins, 1995.

Runestone Press Geography Department. *Sold! The Origins of Money and Trade.* Minneapolis: Lerner Publications, 1994.

Young, Robert. *Money.* Minneapolis: Carolrhoda Books, 1998.

On the Web

For more information about money, use FactHound to track down Web sites related to this book.

1. Go to *www.facthound.com*
2. Type in a search word related to this book or this book ID: 0756504821.
3. Click on the *Fetch It* button.

Your trusty FactHound will fetch the best Web sites for you!

Through the Mail

The American Numismatic Association
Education Department
818 N. Cascade Ave.
Colorado Springs, CO 80903-3279
To get information about coin collecting

On the Road

U.S. Bureau of Engraving and Printing
14th Street and C Street S.W.
Washington, DC 20228
866/874-2330
To see how paper money is printed; tours given May through August

U.S. Mint
320 W. Colfax Ave.
Denver, CO 80204
303/405-4755
To see how coins are made at the U.S. Mint branch in Denver

Index

About the Author

Natalie M. Rosinsky writes about economics, history, science, and other fun things. One of her two cats usually sits on her computer as she works in Mankato, Minnesota. Both cats enjoy pushing coins off tables and playing with dollar bills. Natalie earned graduate degrees from the University of Wisconsin and has been a high school and college teacher.